MW01181660

Cosmic Man

William Kingsland

Kessinger Publishing's Rare Reprints

Thousands of Scarce and Hard-to-Find Books
on These and other Subjects!

- Americana
- Ancient Mysteries
- Animals
- Anthropology
- Architecture
- Arts
- Astrology
- Bibliographies
- Biographies & Memoirs
- Body, Mind & Spirit
- Business & Investing
- Children & Young Adult
- Collectibles
- Comparative Religions
- Crafts & Hobbies
- Earth Sciences
- Education
- Ephemera
- Fiction
- Folklore
- Geography
- Health & Diet
- History
- Hobbies & Leisure
- Humor
- Illustrated Books
- Language & Culture
- Law
- Life Sciences

- Literature
- Medicine & Pharmacy
- Metaphysical
- Music
- Mystery & Crime
- Mythology
- Natural History
- Outdoor & Nature
- Philosophy
- Poetry
- Political Science
- Science
- Psychiatry & Psychology
- Reference
- Religion & Spiritualism
- Rhetoric
- Sacred Books
- Science Fiction
- Science & Technology
- Self-Help
- Social Sciences
- Symbolism
- Theatre & Drama
- Theology
- Travel & Explorations
- War & Military
- Women
- Yoga
- *Plus Much More!*

We kindly invite you to view our catalog list at:
http://www.kessinger.net

THIS ARTICLE WAS EXTRACTED FROM THE BOOK:

Rational Mysticism

BY THIS AUTHOR:

William Kingsland

ISBN 0766151638

READ MORE ABOUT THE BOOK AT OUR WEB SITE:

http://www.kessinger.net

OR ORDER THE COMPLETE
BOOK FROM YOUR FAVORITE STORE
ISBN 0766151638

Because this article has been extracted from a parent book, it may have non-pertinent text at the beginning or end of it.

Any blank pages following the article are necessary for our book production requirements. The article herein is complete.

CHAPTER VI

COSMIC MAN

"I have gone the whole round of creation : I saw and I spoke ;
I, a work of God's hand for that purpose, received in my brain
And pronounced on the rest of His handiwork—returned Him again
His creation's approval or censure : I spoke as I saw :
I report, as a man may of God's work—all's love, yet all's law.
Now I lay down the judgeship He lent me. Each faculty tasked
To perceive Him has gained an abyss, where a dewdrop was asked.
Have I knowledge ? confounded it shrivels at Wisdom laid bare.
Have I forethought ? how purblind, how blank, to the Infinite care !
Do I task any faculty highest, to image success ?
I but open my eyes—and perfection, no more and no less,
In the kind I imagined, full-fronts me, and God is seen God
In the star, in the stone, in the flesh, in the soul and the clod."

BROWNING : Saul.

"I died from the mineral and became a plant ;
I died from the plant and re-appeared in an animal ;
I died from the animal and became a man ;
Wherefore then should I fear ? When did I grow less by dying ?
Next time I shall die from the man
That I may grow the wings of angels.
From the angel, too, must I seek advance ;
'*All things shall perish save His Face.*'
Once more shall I wing my way above the angels ;
I shall become that which entereth not the imagination.
Then let me become naught, naught ; for the harp-string
Crieth unto me ' Verily unto Him do we return ! ' "

JALĀLŪ'D-DĪN RŪMĪ.

CHAPTER VI

COSMIC MAN

CAN we by any possibility, by any of our most daring conceptions, assign to Man in his unitary nature a position and function in the Cosmos, or a relation to the Absolute, or to 'God,' which shall in any degree whatsoever approach that in which he stands in the *reality* of his being and existence? All our deepest intuitions forbid that we should accept that which we *appear* to be, our present limitations, as the *reality* of our nature.

Western tradition sets forth that Man was made in the image and likeness of God; but in the exoteric form of that tradition it has never been realised what is implied thereby. It is only in the esoteric Christian doctrine or Gnôsis, and in the case of a few Christian mystics, that we find any apprehension of the unitary and complementary nature of God and Man— a truth which had been reached ages previously in Eastern tradition, and summarised in the formula, "That art Thou."

Western exoteric tradition, wedded to the literal narrative of Scripture, has riveted its attention on the 'fall' of Man, and has never asked what Man *is* as a unitary Cosmic Being— has never, indeed, taken Man in any unitary sense at all, but has only dealt with Humanity as a succession of individuals, who come into the world from nowhere, and who may or may not be 'saved' by means of a special "favoured-nation" clause when they go out of it again.

If for any it be too high a doctrine that even the individual may claim his oneness with the Absolute; that he never is anything less either in past, present or future, however much *qua* individual he may apparently be separated from his fellows or from Nature, or from spiritual attainment, or limited or dwarfed by the infinities of time and space: then we must necessarily leave that individual to work out his salvation by the light of some less daring, less cosmic conception which may be more in line with the limitations of his intuition, his capacity for abstract thought, or his inherited prejudices.

Such a concept of the divine nature of Man must, indeed, necessarily appear, relatively to Western religious tradition and dogma, to be very much more than too greatly daring. It calls up all sorts of theological bogies, not the least of which is the dreaded spectre of Pantheism, than which nothing is better calculated to send a cold shiver down the adiathermic spine of orthodoxy. Let such, therefore, who cannot face with equanimity the larger view of Man's unity with the Cosmos and the Absolute, remain fixed to their "impregnable rock" of exoteric tradition. There is much safety in such a position, albeit only the safety of the shell-encrusted limpet. Nay, is it not even their high destiny and privilege to be such, in a universe where even limpets, seen in their wholeness, are no more and no less than are humans or gods? Yet let them not think that they will remain limpets for all eternity, however long their desire to remain such will hold them to that state of consciousness. In the course of incalculable ages, even the limpet will be evolved out of all recognition. Still less should they deceive themselves into thinking that the Universe is, or ought to be, all rock and limpet; that in the great ocean of Life in which they are immersed there can be no salvation for any free-swimming creature. Sufficient unto each at each and every moment is the part and lot for which he feels himself fitted; the Great Law will itself carry him on to a larger and fuller life just in proportion as he willingly and gladly co-operates at each step and at each moment by whatsoever his hand or his brain findeth to do.

> " Here is all fulness,
>   Ye brave, to reward you ;
>   Choose well ; your choice is
>   Brief, and yet endless."—GOETHE.

For those who have reached—whether by intuition or otherwise we need not here inquire—a larger view, even that " highest summit of human thought " which the transcendental doctrine presents, and who can, therefore, appreciate a deductive method which makes this its starting-point, we may now advance a few considerations which will place the present facts of Man's evolutionary nature in their broadest light, and will link them up with the concepts of Cosmic Evolution which were stated in our last Chapter, and more particularly with the concept of the Logos.

In doing this let us take leave once and for all of our conventional ideas of great and small, and realise what Emerson has so well expressed in the lines :

"There is no great and no small
To the Soul that maketh all ;
And where it cometh all things are,
And it cometh everywhere."

We shall find that it is our conventional but unreal perception and conception of time and space which is the greatest barrier in the way of a true realisation of the nature of the Self. Is the individual so very small in comparison with the globe on which he lives, that if we do but go a few thousand feet up, our fellow creatures appear to be mere microbes crawling on its surface ? Is our span of life so short that if we take a geological age to be only the equivalent of a single day in the whole history of the Globe, the individual lives merely for a fraction of a second ? Is the Globe itself a mere corpuscle in that larger unit which we call the Solar System ; and the Solar System in its turn a mere atom in the infinitude of worlds and systems which the starry heavens reveal ? Well then, let us look at the reverse picture, at the immeasurable greatness of the individual even when estimated by these common but merely relative standards of time and space.

The most notable achievement of Science during the last twenty years has been to penetrate the hitherto arcane region of the internal structure of the atom of physical matter. This atom is so small in our estimation of the terms small and great, that we are told by Sir J. J. Thompson that if some one had started counting out one atom per second a hundred million years ago, he would not yet have gathered a sufficient number to be detected chemically. Or we may say that it takes about a trillion to make a perceptible speck of matter. From the Newtonian conception of this atom as a " solid, massy, hard, impenetrable particle," which was held almost to the close of last century, physical science has progressed in about twenty years to a concept which sees in it a Solar System in miniature.

It is conceived of as consisting of a central nuclear body corresponding to the Sun, very minute compared with the whole size of the atom, but to which the greatest part of the *mass* of the atom is due. Surrounding this central nucleus are numerous rings or shells of the smaller units now known as *electrons*, which correspond to the Planets—the linear dimensions of these being only about one-hundred-thousandth of the atom itself. If we take the whole Solar System as far as the orbit of Neptune to represent an atom in the Cosmos, the linear dimension of the Earth is only about one three-hundred and fifty-thousandth that of the atom; so that the correspondence is a very close one. The whole atomic system is in a state of intense activity, and the energy confined within its limits is enormous.

Even in his physical body and proportions, then, the individual man, built up of atoms and molecules and cells, is an inconceivable Cosmos of infinite magnitude. If he is infinitely small in one direction, he is infinitely great in the other.

What is the real meaning of these infinite and infinitesimal physical magnitudes—magnitudes which, as it were, cancel each other out in plus and minus? The self, the subject, the ego, stands ever at the centre, and is the zero-point from which all these infinities radiate. The Self is the unit, the unique number *one*: capable of a process—a world-process—of infinite multiplication and of infinite subdivision, but in which the multiplication may equally be regarded as an infinite subdivision, or the subdivision as an infinite multiplication. Shall we, then, abase ourselves before the infinitely great, or exalt ourselves over the infinitely small, as these are apprehended as process in time and space? If we are wise we shall do neither, for they are our own creations. The very fact of their infinitude in either direction, paradoxically deprives them of any validity in abstract thought or transcendental Reality. The consciousness, the subject, the Self which truly apprehends them has already transcended them, and knows itself to be of another order and nature. They are a *how* and not a *what*. Objectively they are manifestations, expressions, appearances, and, more particularly, *limitations* of an infinite, eternal, unborn, self-subsisting LIFE, which is Subject as well as Object, the knower as well as the thing known; and which, knowing Itself as such, knows Itself to be superior to, as well

as active in these Appearances. They should have no power
to spell-bind us in their mere *physical* proportions. The
infinitely great is just as much a limitation as the infinitely
small. Why should *magnitudes* of any kind move us to degrees
of emotion, or wonderment, or awe, or fear ? Is there any
more cause for these in the immensity of the starry heavens
than in the commonest material object which we daily and
momentarily contact ? The cause for silent adoration lies not
in the outward appearance or size of the object, but in the
thought of the Root or Ground of its being ; the One Eternal
Infinite Power by and through and in which the humblest
flower, or blade of grass, or " tip of Autumn spikelet " exists,
and is brought into manifestation equally with the universe
of Suns and Stars. We are deluded by mere *appearance* if
we go no deeper than the outward fact ; nor shall we ever
apprehend *truth* until we have freed ourselves from this illusion
of magnitude.

The wonderment does not lie in the degree of the fact,
but in the fact itself—the great fact that the Universe is not
a mechanism but a LIFE, and that we *are* that LIFE. The real
cause of all emotion—whether it be the exquisite dawn of love
in youth or maiden, or the intense fervour of creative genius,
the ideal of the poet, the artist, or the philosopher, or whether
it be the religious fervour of the saint, or the rapt ecstasy of
the mystic—lies in the fact that it is the revelation of the Self
to the self, the great discovery by the individual self of the
potentiality of its own infinite nature. Perchance we find
here, as some have thought, the *cause* of all this manifested
drama in time and space. " To taste of reality and illusion,
the great Self becomes twofold." [1]

The discovery is made by the individual self *first* as a
rapport with something which appears to be a separate entity,
an *object* of desire, of love ; but afterwards it becomes a *union*
in which the distinction of subject and object is lost ; and in
that union is found the supremest freedom, the supremest
love, and thereby also the supremest bliss.

The movement of Suns and Planets and Star Systems is no
greater fact than the movement of my little finger. Millions
of microcosmic systems come into and go out of existence
with each breath that I draw. THAT which I am, and THAT

[1] *Maitri Upanishad*, 7, 11. Deusen's trans.

which the starry heavens reveal in their own manner and degree, are one and the same LIFE. Do you think that it is any greater thing for 'God' to act in the infinite Cosmos than it is for you to act in your own body? The chemist wishing to demonstrate the properties of a substance, does not need many tons for his purpose : a few grains are all that he requires. Is there any greater wonder, when we consider the fact itself, in the explosion of a hundred tons of gunpowder than there is in the explosion of a single grain? The fact of being able to know, to see, to feel, to think, to love, is the great mystical fact, in no wise altered by any degree of it, though the degree may and does serve commonly, and in the first instance, to bring the fact more vividly into realisation for the individual self. When rightly and philosophically appreciated, the infinities lose for us their artificial extensive values ; they disclose to us our own illimitable nature, and we enter into that revelation with an exultant faith in an infinite Perfection, and the unspeakable joy of a realised Freedom.

"Verily, he who has seen, heard, comprehended, and known the Self, by him is this entire universe known."[1]

There is still a further reason why we should not allow these physical magnitudes to limit our concepts as to the real nature of our being. It is because they *are* simply physical magnitudes ; because they belong only to that furthest plane of differentiation and apparent separation which we term physical matter, or physical consciousness, and have no validity in the deeper strata of our being, or in what we more generally speak of as the 'higher' planes of consciousness. They are almost wholly non-existent on the psychic plane, and practically entirely absent on the mental plane. This is a matter of actual experience and evidence in connection with psychical research, and is as verifiable as any other scientific fact ; though it must be remembered that many scientific facts, even of a physical nature, are unverifiable by the individual without special qualifications and long and arduous training. But in the light of our fundamental principle of the Cosmic nature of the Self, and the unity of the individual self with the Cosmic Self, it is not difficult to accept the evidence of psychical research, and the further evidence of certain mystics, that when freed from the limitations of the physical

---

[1] *Brihad-āranyaka Upanishad*, 2.4. 5b. Deusen's trans.

senses, time and space are largely or entirely transcended, and their magnitudes disappear. When thus freed, we say that the self—the individual self—is acting on the psychic plane or the mental plane, as the case may be ; though it may be doubted whether psychical research is as yet cognisant of any phenomena deeper than the psychic plane. What it is important to realise is, that the self does actually possess an appropriate body or vehicle for, and exists on, each and all of the planes, however many there may be ; they are part of our cosmic wholeness, and we have our life and action on these planes *now*, and not merely when we part from our physical body at death. Were it not so we could have no existence, no life, or functions, or thought, or consciousness on this 'lower' or physical plane, any more than the physical atom could exist, or have mass, or inertia, or energy, apart from its etheric nature and existence, its unity with the one Substance. To pass in consciousness from the limitations of the physical plane to the comparative freedom of the psychic plane, and from thence to the still greater freedom of the mental plane, and so to whatsoever higher or deeper plane there may be, is merely to fall back upon our own cosmic nature, the depths of our own being ; upon a 'self' which at each step becomes less and less individual and separate, and more and more cosmic in its unitary nature ; until, in the supreme mystical experience and ecstasy, we 'become' that which we always *are*—the One Absolute Self.

Neither Subject nor Object is primary. That which is both Subject and Object we call the Absolute, and its primary *aspects*—which in the conceptual mind are a duality —we designate Principle and Substance : Principle being the universal omnipresent potentiality of every individual subject, whilst Substance is the potentiality of all and every individual object or form which, under the category of *time*, appears first of all non-spatially as Idea or Logos, and subsequently as the manifested universe of Matter extended in space. Every single object, we have already seen, *is* the One Substance, and therefore contains the infinite potentiality of form which that Substance contains in its infinite nature. But the infinite potentiality for form which Substance contains is, in its other aspect, the infinite potentiality for Idea : which potentiality we arbitrarily separate as belonging to Subject in distinction from Object. Every individual object, then, is not merely in its real nature infinite Object, but also infinite Subject ; for the two are one. But it does not manifest this absoluteness, for if it did so there would be no universe of infinite variety. Its very nature and function *qua* individual is to manifest in part only, and so to create a universe in which separation, extension, and process, is law and necessity.

This is somewhat quaintly expressed by the author of the *Theologia Germanica* as follows :

" All this resteth in God as a substance but not as a working, so long as there is no creature. And out of this expressing and revealing of Himself to Himself, ariseth the distinction of Persons. . . . And without the creature, this would lie in His own Self as a Substance or well-spring, but would not be manifested or wrought out in deeds. Now God will have it to be exercised and clothed in a form, for it is there only to be wrought out and exercised. What else is it for ? Shall it lie idle ? What, then, would it profit ? As good were it that it had never been ; nay, better, for what is of no use existeth in vain, and that is abhorred by God and Nature. However, God will have it wrought out, and this cannot come to pass (which it ought to do) without the creature. Nay, if there ought not to be, and were not this and that—works, and a world full of real things, and the like— what were God Himself, and what had He to do, and whose God would He be ? " [1]

It is clearly seen that individualisation—the coming into existence of the ' creature '—takes place by a process of limitation which is more or less in the nature of an illusion ; and this we may assign for the sake of clearness to the *subjective* nature of the individual object, be it atom, man, or god. We have further located this limiting process in what we know as Mind : in Cosmic Mind in the first instance, creating certain Cosmic differentiations which subjectively are great Cosmic Beings, creative Potencies, or Gods ; and objectively, or substantially, are Planes of Substance and Cosmic Bodies. On each Plane a repetition of this process takes place, down to the smallest atom, so that the same law, the same principle of unity in diversity, applies to each part as well as to the Whole.

It is not merely true that individualisation is necessarily limitation, and also that without that limitation there could be no universe of infinite variety, or of any variety at all ; but it is equally true from another point of view that the individual

[1] *Theologia Germanica,* chap. xxxi.

must, to a very large extent, be dependent upon this limitation of consciousness for the proper performance of his individual function in the Whole. The individual is inhibited by Nature from any further degree of consciousness or knowledge than such as is immediately required for his place and function in the economy of the Whole. The immediate function of the individual—whether individual atom or individual man—is *action* in a certain definite manner. For that purpose it, or he, is shut out from all immediate consciousness of any environment other than that in which and upon which he is to act and react ; it is that, and that only, which forms his ' world.' From this point of view we may regard organism as being not so much in the nature of an aid to consciousness, as an instrument for the limitation thereof. Who is there with any *faith* who does not expect an immeasurably enhanced consciousness and knowledge when free from the limitations of the physical body ? Such an enhanced consciousness, indeed, when the physical senses are inhibited, is already a well-recognised fact in psychology.

But the individual is not absolutely and entirely shut out from the whole content of Infinity with which, as an environment, he acts and reacts, and which, as a *reality*, is the infinite content of his own Self. If he were absolutely shut out, there could never be any consciousness of a *beyond*, of anything in any way transcending immediate environment. Always and ever there is an irradiation of the so-called actual from a transcendental region, the region of the ideal ; this being the more or less consciously felt influence of the infinite *Potential* of the Absolute ; and to it is due the great push of evolution. The tiniest atom feels it ; for the atom *is* the infinite Potential as well as the limited actual. And if now it is only given to the atom, or to any lesser or greater individual as we reckon small and great, to be thus limited and restricted, it is also given to it to feel and to hear in a manner which must always be *mystical*—as being inexplicable in the categories of the actual and empirical to which the individual for the time being belongs—the silent, invisible, yet irresistible call and attraction of the Infinite Potential, which, in that very attraction, confers upon the individual the power to respond to It, and to expand even to Its own infinite and immeasurable richness and fulness of Life.

Let us clearly realise that the potential must be as existent as that which we call the actual; it is only potential and unmanifested in so far that it exists beyond the plane of our present perceptions, our present action and function. Potential energy is just as much a reality and an activity as kinetic energy; it exists somewhere and is active somewhere. In the case of physical energy we may at least relegate it to the etheric plane.[1] If I do or become a certain thing, it is because I possess the capacity for doing or becoming that thing; that is to say, the capacity to do or become it is part of my nature, part of myself. It is just as much in existence, just as much a reality before the actual doing or becoming, as it is in the present action, or after the action.

The human germ-cell, a mere speck about the one-hundred-and-twentieth part of an inch in diameter, contains the potentiality of evolving into the completely organised human being; and biologists would fain discover in the structure of that cell —or rather in the structure of the nucleus of that cell—the cause of heredity as well as of variation.[2] There is certainly plenty of room in that minute cell for unlimited variations of structure; for it is itself a mighty cosmos of the microcosmic solar systems which we call atoms. We may, in fact, readily admit that individual variations of structure, corresponding to that which subsequently evolves therefrom, do exist; but that the *causes* of heredity or variation lie in the structure, we must deny on the same terms that we must deny that the cause of any physical structure lies in the structure itself, at any period whatsoever of its existence. Always and ever we have to seek deeper and still deeper for causes; and there is no term until we have reached the Absolute. Whether it be the formation of an atom or of a human germ-cell, the whole potentiality of the Absolute goes to its making, and is latent— another convenient fiction—therein. It is merely convention or convenience which necessitates that we should stop short at any more proximate cause. We may say that the human germ-cell becomes a full-grown man of a definite type and not any other animal, because of a certain definite structure of the germ-cell; but physical organism *qua* organism is—in so far as it can *manifest* anything—merely the capacity to respond more or less definitely to certain cosmic forces. These forces

---

[1] Cf. *Scientific Idealism*, p. 79.   [2] *Ibid.*, p. 266.

are everywhere ; at every point of space exists the whole living
potentiality of the Absolute ; but the atom, or the man, or the
god, will only manifest so much of it as, in his form-limitation
qua atom, man, or god he can respond to. And if materialists
and empiricists would have us think that consciousness is
merely response to external stimuli or environment : we shall
ask them, Where does external stimulus or environment begin
or end ? Every plane acts and reacts with every other plane ;
the very principle of the unity of Nature—and Nature cannot
now, in the light of our scientific knowledge, be restricted to the
physical plane—makes all Nature our environment.

When Sir J. J. Thompson states that " all mass is mass of
the ether, all momentum, momentum of the ether, all kinetic
energy, kinetic energy of the ether," [1] he is not merely stating
a physical fact, but also unconsciously enunciating the great
fundamental principle that all phenomena whatsoever are
only special cases of the activity of Root Substance, however
many planes there may be beyond the etheric.

Even now, in our physical bodies, we possess powers of
conscious response to cosmic forces which do not act through
our ordinary sense organs. We possess inner senses which we
utterly neglect, and the existence of which many are foolish
enough to deny *a priori* when evidenced by others, because
forsooth they have no experience of them in their own limited
nature. Psychical research shows us that both the past and
the future may become objectively present in our consciousness ; and that it is as possible to see an object on the other
side of the world as it is to see one in our own immediate
vicinity.

If we *must* talk in terms of time and space, of great and
small, of existence and becoming : let us at least recognise that
the true nature of a thing, its true *greatness*, is only discoverable
in its inner nature and relations, not in its outer size, function,
or form ; for the outer measure and relationship of the thing
is always dwarfed by something greater, and still greater
again, until, in relation to infinity, a Solar System becomes as
infinitely small as an atom. But when we consider the inner
nature and relations of a thing, the thing itself, however small
it may be, expands to infinity, and itself becomes the Infinite.
It is then found to be the one infinite Substance, with the

[1] *Electricity and Matter*, p. 51.

potentiality of all that ever was, is, or will be—that potentiality being infinitely more *real* than the fragmentary portion which we are pleased to call the actual *present*. The Cosmos is not great because of its outer expansion in diversity, but because of its inner compaction in Unity; or shall we say that it is great in both aspects when we view these as complementary modes of the ONE LIFE; the outer being but a reflection of the inner in opposite terms; the infinite object corresponding to the infinite subject, the infinite multiplicity to the infinite Unity.

There is just as much room for 'me,' on the potential side, in an atom as in a germ-cell; and, indeed, we have heard of a 'permanent atom' as the starting-point of the physical development of the individual. Weismann would have us believe in the continuity of the germ-plasm—the germinal cell of one individual being derived in a direct line of ancestral descent from germ-cell to germ-cell. Whatever of truth or otherwise there may be in this theory, what we wish to enforce here is, that so far as size is concerned it does not matter whether the continuity is preserved in a single atom or in a single biaphore containing billions of atoms; the one is just as capable of becoming a human being as the other, for it has behind it the whole potentiality of the Absolute, but is nevertheless determined as to its immediate development by local conditions and limitations. Thus although I am in the totality of my being never anything less than the Absolute, I am limited as an individual manifestation both by the organism in or through which I am manifesting—be it atom, germ-cell, or full-grown body—and also by a local environment which belongs to some larger or more cosmic unit constituting the *nature* of the species to which I belong, or the plane of Substance out of which my body or vehicle is formed. Whilst I am thus limited by organism, I limit myself also in consciousness; I think of myself as individual and separate, and what I think, that I empirically am. Yet even while I am thus affirming myself to be individual atom, or man, or god, I am at the same time negating my affirmation. The very affirmation of a limitation or individualisation is the negation of that limitation by implication of a larger something which is affirmed as being that of, or from, or in which the limitation takes place, and to which it bears a relation. The One Self is necessarily negation as well as affirmation. The Self in action continually affirms, ' I am this, and this, and this.' But ever there is the eternal negation, ' I am not this, and this, and this—" neti, neti "—for I am also its opposite, and I am always more than any individual thing, and still more, and infinitely more, and there is nothing that can contain and limit me.' Thus in the *Bhagavad-Gita* we find Krishna (the Logos) saying :

> " I am the Ego which is seated in the hearts of all beings ; I am the beginning, the middle, and the end of all existing things. . . . I am, O Arjuna, the seed of all existing things, and there is not anything, whether animate or inanimate, which is without me. My divine manifestations, O harasser of thy foes, are without end." [1]

We may now clearly apprehend that in the world of action of our present consciousness, in which the fundamental principle is duality, opposition, affirmation, negation : there exists not merely the duality of subject and object, or self and not-self, but also a duality in each constituent of this fundamental duality ; for in the object or not-self we have the duality of substance and form, or matter, which, *qua* matter, apparently possesses a nature of its own ; and we have in the subject the duality of the One Self and the individual self ; the latter thinking itself a separate entity or ego, and in fact always acting as such in the immediate field of its activity or environment.

It is convenient to refer to these two aspects of the One Self as the higher or cosmic, and the lower or individual self ; or simply to distinguish the one as the *Self* and the other as the self. The distinction is as arbitrary and empirical as that between atom and substance ; but then all distinctions of language are such : they necessarily express an either-or in a universe in which the law of *action* is differentiation and opposition. The function of the lower or individual self is to be to the higher or Cosmic Self what the atom, or the cell, or the organ is to the larger unit or body of which it is a part. The law is always multiplicity within unity. But if the atom, or the cell, or the organ were in actual consciousness anything *more* than that which they are in their individual nature, how could or would they effectively fulfil their limited function ? The *more* exists as a latent potentiality ; and in Man it becomes more or less clearly recognised and defined as the hope of attainment of an ideal and infinite perfection. How, indeed,

[1] Chap. x, 20, 39, 40.

can we conceive it to be otherwise than that that which has gone out from the ONE—or *appears* to have done so—should return thereto ? Such a *return* is not merely the root of all religion, but it is what we actually recognise in the world-process as we at present know it, or what is commonly called evolution : which is at root an expansion of life and consciousness acting in or through more and more highly organised physical forms.

But that such an expansion should take place at all, there must have been a previous limitation or involution—an in-volution of life or spirit, an e-volution of matter or form—and we have already outlined our conception of the Cosmic Process as a whole as being such an evolution of matter and form followed by a devolution of these and a return to Spirit or Unity. In minor cycles within the great universal cycle we may find both of these movements in operation. Worlds and systems evolve and devolve in, and out of, the One Substance.

In all these fundamental distinctions of Substance and Matter, Self and Not-self, God and Man, Higher Self and lower self : we may recognise that the relation and function is the same in each and every case. What the Absolute or ' God ' is to Cosmic Man, so is the Higher Self to the lower self ; and it is only as we discover, realise, and solve that great mystery within our individual selves, that we can do so also for the Cosmos as a whole. For in very fact what we call the Cosmos as a whole—as if it were something outside of and immeasurably greater than ourselves—is entirely and wholly within the illimitable limits of our own being and consciousness.

When we look at the evolution of Man, or Humanity as a whole, on this Globe, we find that the distinguishing feature of that evolution within the periods of which we have any knowledge, is the gradual attainment of the power to recognise the cosmic nature of the Self as well as the individual nature of the self. This power rises from feeble beginnings, as religious aspiration, or philosophical intuition, to a higher degree, if not yet to its fullest fruition, in Mysticism.[1] We attribute

---

[1] In Mr. Edward Carpenter's work, *Pagan and Christian Creeds : their Origin and Meaning*, three stages of this evolution are distinguished as (1) Simple Consciousness, (2) Self Consciousness, and (3) Universal Consciousness. This latter is the *mystical* consciousness which has not yet dawned for the great majority of the race.

this power in the first instance to the evolution of what we call Mind. That there should be a concomitant evolution of organic structure in the brain, the instrument of mind, is not merely to be expected, but is the only condition under which any such development of mind could manifest itself on the physical plane. There must be the corresponding organ, or basis of manifestation, on whatsoever plane the Self is acting. In other words, the Self must have a *body* in order to *manifest* on any plane whatsoever. But the Self which possesses the potentiality of that manifestation is no more attributable to the body or vehicle than the potentiality of mass, momentum, or kinetic energy in the atom is attributable to the structure of the atom. The structure of the atom will admit of just so much manifestation of that cosmic potentiality—attributed as we have seen to the nature of the ether—as will admit of its being an atom of a specific kind, and no more ; and the same principle holds good whether the individual be an atom, a cell, a plant, an animal, a man, or a god.

If the physical evolution of a man dates from a germ-cell —or perchance even earlier, from a single atom—it is equally certain that we must trace back the physical evolution of the Race to the earliest appearance of any form of organised life on this Globe, and even to the mineral kingdom itself. Behind the glowing mass of nebulous matter constituting this Globe in the early stages of its existence, lay the potentiality of evolving the vegetable, the animal, and the human kingdoms, up to Man as we at present know him physically. In each and every case this potentiality only lay *in* matter in the sense that matter only manifests in varying degrees and with varying characteristics that which exists in the potentiality of *Substance* on higher or more cosmic planes ; whilst behind the potentiality of Substance, as the root or noumenon of matter or object, lies the eternal potentiality of Consciousness or Subject as the inseparable correlative therewith.

Even if we are to think of the evolutionary process as Bergson would have us think of it, as a continual creation of something absolutely new in virtue of the ever-presence of the whole potentiality of the past : that *whole* ever growing or " swelling " in some occult manner by feeding on itself : shall we not still have to postulate that it has already had an Infinity in which to swell, and that therefore its content or

potentiality must be infinite ?   The infinite fulness and richness
of this potentiality is, therefore, the same, whether we regard
it in this light, or whether we regard it in the light of an
Absolute which needs no such process in order to become what
IT eternally IS.   In any case the potentiality does not lie in
matter as such, but in the Cosmos as a whole : that is to say
in *Substance*, not in its phenomenal forms.

Looking at cosmic evolution as a whole, or looking merely
at the evolution of this Globe where cosmic principles are
repeated—as indeed they are in the evolution of any single
atom—we may now ask ourselves more definitely : What
position does Man collectively—Humanity in its totality of
past, present and future—occupy in relation to the whole
process ?   The position which we assign to him in succession
to the mineral, the vegetable, and the animal kingdoms is
a purely arbitrary one.   We say that the human germ-cell
is *human* from the very earliest stages to which we can trace
it.   We know that the stages of its development are a recapitu-
lation of the larger cosmic stages of the evolution of living
forms on this Globe.   May we not then enlarge our concept
of Man as a cosmic being at least to this extent, that what
the individual germ-cell is to the individual man, so is the
cosmic germ-cell—that is to say the primordial form and stages
of evolution of this Globe—to Cosmic Man ?   This Planet
is a Man-bearing Planet ; it cannot be considered in this
connection otherwise than as the field of evolution of Man.
But our fundamental principles forbid us to conceive of any
such field of evolution otherwise than as an integral part of the
constitution of Man, the evolving entity itself ; for subject
and object are inseparable.   That which cuts us off from an
appreciation of this unitary nature of Man and his environment,
is simply our lack of knowledge and understanding of the
action and interaction of the deeper and more universal planes,
on which Man exists in a more unitary manner than on the
physical plane.   The whole evolution of this Globe is
indissolubly connected with the evolution of Cosmic Man on
a plane of consciousness which at present we term the physical ;
and however far back we may go in the embryo history of the
Globe, we are dealing with a corresponding history of the
physical evolution of Man.

There is every reason to believe—whether by analogy, or

by the authority of the ancient traditions embodied in the Scriptures of various Religions—that there are other orders of Beings in the Cosmos besides Man; and each of these will have their appropriate field of evolution. We shall thereby assign to the Sun and Planets an appropriate Cosmic Life which, in its individual aspect as Sun or Planet, will be a Being of which the physical body or Globe is the expression on the physical plane. There is no single physical unit without a *soul*; for every physical thing exists on all the planes of the universe. The 'World-Soul' is MAN; and in and through MAN the whole evolution of this Globe takes place.

But we must carry the principle of Unity in diversity still further. This Earth is only one of a number of Worlds or Globes all dependent upon the Sun for their life and energy. The Solar System is in itself a Cosmic Unit, and as such must have a unitary LIFE. It might be convenient to call that Life a Logos. The principle of correspondence and analogy must serve us here in the great as in the small. Individual man is the Logos for his own body, that body being macrocosmic relatively to the individual. Cosmic Man is the Logos for his own Globe. The Solar Logos stands in the same relation to the whole of His System; and however much further afield we may go into the Cosmos, we must consider that each smaller unit is comprised within some larger one, until we have reached—though we never can reach it in this manner—the one Supreme Logos of the whole Manifested Universe.

Let us not forget that this *extension* is our intellectual apprehension of the matter. By intuition we realise that in a certain sense it is pure illusion, and that of that Supreme Logos—and even of the 'lesser' ones; aye, even of Man himself—it must be said :

"Where it cometh all things are,
And it cometh everywhere."

In the Consciousness of the Supreme Logos, Man, together with all other Cosmic Beings, must constitute a Unity which not merely as a whole, but also in each of its parts, must stand in its complete perfection of purpose and function, the complete fulfilment of the Eternal *Idea*.

If, then, we ask why Man appears to us to have 'fallen,' why Humanity now appears to be such an imperfect, weak, necessitous, erring, ignorant, suffering being ? : the reply will be, in the first place, that we do not see Man in his Wholeness ; and in the second place that this ' fall ' was necessary in order that he might fulfil his cosmic function.

We only see a minute fragment of Man, either in what he is historically—that is to say as an evolving unitary being—or in what he is eternally in his spiritual wholeness and perfection, " made in the image of God."

Historically, we only know of Man during the very limited period of a few thousand years. Scientifically, we must assign to him millions of years during which he has existed and will continue to exist on this Globe. In the vast evolutionary time-process of our Earth, Man appears to us superficially to be a mere succession of individuals, with no particular function in the economy of Nature or of the cosmic process as a whole. In the course of incalculable ages he has evolved physically from the lowest forms of Protozoa. Each individual man evolves thus to-day ; repeating in the short space of nine months the whole evolutionary history of the Race from that point. We may go still further back to physical matter itself, in which we do not as yet scientifically recognise any form of life, though it must necessarily be as *potential* in the atom as in the protozoa. In the course of incalculable ages still to come, Man may, and doubtless will, evolve a physical body which will be as unlike his present body as the body of a horse to-day is unlike the five-toed animal somewhat resembling a small fox from which we can trace his direct descent. Among other things it is highly probable that before Man has finished his evolution on this Globe, the physical separation of the sexes will have vanished. These are matters, however, which cannot be decided from any scientific knowledge which we at present possess ; whilst the information which is given in certain occult schools would be out of place here. I have, however, shown in *Scientific Idealism* [1] that Man is the parent stem of the great Tree of Life on this Globe—the animals having evolved from Man, and not Man from the animals. The present animals are collateral descendants from the intermediate types or species which, in this definitely directed evolution, formed the direct line or parent stem of Man's genealogical tree. Present physical man has evolved through the animal Kingdom, as

[1] Chap. xiii.

also through the still earlier vegetable and mineral; so that in *physical* history these Kingdoms come first. Every individual man, in his pre-natal development in the womb, evolves through these lower Kingdoms; but yet we call the embryo *human*, even its very earliest stages, when it is recapitulating the evolution of the *animal* Kingdom.

If we could see Man in his wholeness on the more inner planes of the Cosmos, we should find a still closer connection between him and the material world in which he functions; we should in fact see Man as the creator of his own world. If we see and know Man now only in such a fragmentary manner on the horizontally extended line of the evolutionary time-process, it is equally certain that we see and know even less of him on the vertical line of his direct connection with the Absolute; that is to say, in his existence and functions on the deeper and more universal and unitary planes of the Cosmos

Consider well that even physically we see but a fragmentary part of any individual man, and—save in exceptional cases hardly as yet credited—nothing at all of his actual existence on the higher planes of Substance or Consciousness. How much the more is it true that we see and know but an infinitesimal part of Cosmic Man in his whole nature, extending through every plane up to the Supreme Logos. If we could see and know the whole of any individual man, we should see and know Cosmic Man; and if we saw and knew Cosmic Man, we should see and know the Logos; and to see and know the Logos, the ' Son,' is to see and know the ' Father,' the Absolute. This is only carrying to its logical conclusion in the connection between Life and Matter, or Subject and Object, what Science has already recognised for Matter only; for Lord Kelvin tells us that :

" All the properties of matter are so connected that we can scarcely imagine one *thoroughly explained*, without our seeing its relation to all the others; without, in fact, having the explanation of all." [1]

If, then, we could know Man in his wholeness and completeness; if we could know him " in spirit and in truth " : should we not have to recognise that in spite of the nescience, the imperfection, the ' evil ' of that fragmentary part of him which is all that is immediately present in our consciousness, his

[1] *Popular Lectures and Addresses*, Art. " Constitution of Matter."

wholeness and completeness constitutes a divine perfection of Truth, Goodness, and Beauty of inconceivable richness and infinite fulness ?

This question admits of no other than an affirmative answer from those who take it as a primary and fundamental postulate that the Absolute, or God, is in Itself or Himself such an Absolute and Infinite Perfection, and at the same time is ' All and in All.'

The syllogism may be stated thus :

God is Absolute Perfection.
God is the Universe in its Wholeness and Unity.
Therefore the Universe in its Wholeness is Absolute Perfection.

We can only deny this by denying or qualifying either the major or the minor premise. It is possible to postulate an imperfect Absolute, an Absolute ' in the making.' But this is a spurious Absolute which never emerges from the time-process. It is a counsel of despair of the formal mind. It has never been the mystic's Absolute, nor that of any great Religion. We shall cease to believe at the peril of our sanity in an eternal divine Perfection at the root and source of all things. All that is deepest and strongest in us leads us to believe in such a Perfection. But the perfection of the whole implies the perfection of the part. It implies the perfection of the Logos as the *Idea* of the manifested Cosmos ; and it implies the perfection of Man *now* in *his* wholeness and completeness, however imperfect the fragmentary parts may appear to be. In a perfect Whole every part must be perfect. The measure and standard of the perfection of a part is the proper fulfilling or exercise of its function in the whole ; and dare we affirm, with our fragmentary and imperfect knowledge of Man, that he does not fulfil that function ? Even the Devil must be conceived of as perfect in his part and function in the Cosmos. We call many things in Nature vile ; but are they vile to the One Life which lives and moves in them just as much as in us ? Our empirical consciousness tells us that Man is sinful and imperfect ; but our intuition, and even our logical faculty, tells us that whether as the ' creation ' of a perfect God, as being the image and likeness of such a God ; or whether in another aspect Man can claim to be, in the wholeness of his nature, nothing short of the Absolute itself : He must necessarily be as perfect as the God who ' creates ' him, or as the Absolute which he *is*. Thus, quite apart from Mysticism, we find that this conclusion may be arrived at philosophically. Professor Royce arrives at this conclusion as the result of a close and rationalistic analysis of the meaning of the concept *Being*. He says :

" All finite life is a struggle with evil. Yet from the final point of view the Whole is good. The Temporal Order contains at no one moment anything that can satisfy. Yet the Eternal Order is perfect. We have all sinned, and come short of the glory of God. Yet in just our life, viewed in its entirety, the glory of God is completely manifest. These hard sayings are the deepest expressions of the essence of true religion. They are also the most inevitable outcome of philosophy. . . . In the bare assertion of just these truths, that appear to our ordinary consciousness a stumbling-block and foolishness, the wisest of humanity, in India, in Greece, and in the history of Christian thought, are agreed." [1]

The reconciliation of an empirical sense of evil with the intuition of an absolute Good is only a part of the general problem of the intellect in its inability to reach the ' thing in itself.' We have to make our choice between empiricism or materialism as giving us a true perception of things in their *reality*, and the idealism or intuition which looks to a trans-cendental perfection only partially discovered or manifested in external things of our present consciousness. We have already made our choice ; and, indeed, we see most clearly that the evolutionary process is itself one in which empiricism is continually being jettisoned, and the ideal brought into the region of the real.

Professor Edward Caird has a very illuminative view of this question in a passage in his work on *The Evolution of Religion*.[2]

" The thought of a God who *externally* dominates over the course of nature and history is a compromise which cannot permanently be maintained. In the long run, a religion based on such a conception must advance to the idea of a spiritual principle which is immanent in the object as it is in the subject, or else it must carry the opposition of the subject to the object to the point at which the latter is con-templated as purely evil or negative. That which is outside of God

---

[1] *The World and the Individual*, vol. ii, p. 379.
[2] Vol. ii, p. 63. 1893 ed.

is necessarily that which is opposed to Him, and that which is opposed to the divine must be evil, so far as it can be regarded as having any positive existence at all. We may illustrate this process of thought by the development of the Kantian philosophy as it is shown on the one side in the pessimism of Schopenhauer, and, on the other side, in the optimism of Schelling and Hegel. The former is the necessary result, if Kant's first tendency to oppose reason to sense, and consequently the subject to the object, be insisted on, and carried out to its consequences. This opposition forces Kant himself to conceive the realisation of the moral idea as a *Progressus ad infinitum* ; but even infinite time is not enough for the impossible task of uniting the moral with the natural, the sensuous desires with the law of reason. Hence it was open to Schopenhauer to argue that they could not be united at all. On the other hand, if we admit the postulate of Kant, that the moral idea *must* be realised, and if we go on with him to recognise, as he recognises in the *Critique of Judgment* and the *Essay on the Idea of Universal History*, that in a sense it is realised already, or is progressively realising itself in nature and history, then we must advance beyond Kant in a different direction. We must reduce the opposition between sense and reason, or between consciousness and self-consciousness to a *relative* opposition, which exists in order that it may be transcended. In other words, we must adopt something like the evolutionary optimism of Hegel."

Cosmic Man exists on all the planes of the Cosmos, and in an appropriate manner fulfils his function thereon. If Man appears to be individual and fragmentary on the physical plane, he must appear to be less so on the psychic plane, and still less so on the mental plane, whilst on the spiritual plane we can only postulate that he exists in his eternal perfection as the unitary Man, " made in the image of God."

Shall that image be less perfect, less complete than that which it manifests ? Even if it manifests in part only, that part must necessarily be perfect as part of a perfect Whole. That part or image exists as the Logos ; and if spiritual Man has fallen, then has the Logos Himself fallen. Doubtless there is a sense in which Man has fallen, and a corresponding sense also in which the Logos has fallen ; but in the latter case we do not call it a ' fall,' we call it ' the mystery of the Incarnation.' We cannot resolve that mystery with the intellect any more than we can resolve the mystery of apparent individualism and separation in a fundamental Unity, or an apparent evil in a fundamental or absolute Good. We say that these are appearances not Reality, and we strive ever to apprehend the Reality underlying the appearance. But this much at least we can apprehend, that in each and every case where we say, in the conventional language of the formal mind, that the Unity *becomes* a multiplicity, or *appears* in separation and opposition : the fundamental Unity is in no wise thereby in any sense divided ; it still *remains* in all its absoluteness.   The Ether does not cease to be Ether, *qua* Ether, when it differentiates into physical matter ; and more-over it is only the minutest portion of the whole Ether which thus differentiates.   Cosmic Mind does not cease to be Cosmic Mind, as such, when a portion of it differentiates into individual minds ; nor can we conceive in any manner that it is thereby, so to speak, emptied of its content.   The spiritual plane is not emptied to make the lower planes, nor is spiritual Man emptied that Man may exist on the lower planes.   All these are *appearances* ; and we can take our choice as to whether we will continue to view the Universe in this fragmentary manner, or whether we will make the unitary Reality our permanent and all-embracing standpoint.

How can anyone have a due appreciation either of his own nature or of the nature of ' God ' when he views Man only in the limited and fragmentary manner of the individual ; and can even imagine that the relation of God to Man is mostly connected with the ' salvation ' of a comparatively few in-dividual selves or fragments which are necessarily impermanent, which are *appearance* only, and which can never be ' saved ' until they have themselves determined to be ' lost ' in the eternal reality of the ONE ?

" Then the man says : ' Behold ! I, poor fool that I was, imagined that it was I, but behold ! it is, and was, of a truth, God ! ' " [1]

Man has come out or ' fallen ' from his spiritual estate, yet he remains there in his divine perfection.   His fall is his mission and function in the Cosmos ; and the Cosmos is a manifestation of an eternally existing divine perfection.   There can be no final perfectibility in an infinite time-process regarded as always adding something more to an imperfection.   The only sense in which the time-process can be regarded as leading to a final perfection is in the attainment of a fulness of consciousness of an already existing perfection from which the individual is

[1] *Theologia Germanica,* chap. v.

temporarily shut out in order that he may fulfil his necessary function in the Cosmos. Thus the individual can only attain to perfection by knowing what he *is* in his oneness with the Perfect. Imperfection is in limitation of consciousness, not in the fulness of the Eternal Reality. And may we not say that long before we reach that fulness of realisation we shall have assuredly discovered that for every pang we have suffered in this so-called evil world, there is compensation a million-fold ; that " our light affliction *which is but for a moment* worketh for us a far more exceeding and eternal weight of glory "? We attain to perfection and are ' saved ' only by attaining to " the full-grown man, unto the measure of the stature of the fulness of Christ," the Logos, the Cosmic Man, who has ' fallen ' or ' incarnated,' has been crucified on the Cross of Matter, yet remains as the perfect manifestation of the ever-concealed Causeless-Cause.

But we cannot attain to this *fulness* as the result of any outward growth ; it is the opening up of our inner conscious-ness ; an expansion inwards in that ' direction ' in which every individualised ' thing ' becomes more and more universal. All ' sin,' all ' evil ' thus resolves itself into a cherished sense of egoity or separateness ; and the more a man seeks to preserve that sense of egoity the more he is lost to the realisation of the illimitable fulness and perfection of his eternal and immortal nature. That perfection stands in its wholeness and complete-ness in the consciousness of the Logos, the Cosmic God-Man— even as a process the end being complete from the beginning— and it does not appear to be beyond the power of the individual to reach some such unitary consciousness even now, whilst still in a physical body. The attainment of this unitary consciousness is Mysticism ; or perhaps we should rather say, that in so far as there is a mystic ' Way ' to be travelled before the realisation is actually attained, Mysticism is the effort to attain. The mystic may be at various stages of the Way, but we shall still call him a mystic, because the goal is clearly realised as attainable ; because he has set out to climb to the very summit of the Mount of Transfiguration, whilst others merely walk vainly round and round the base.

Mysticism is the fruition of religion, but it is also a distinct departure from it as religion is commonly understood and practised. Mysticism **may be said** to commence as soon as the individual commences to perceive his unitive nature, to perceive his indissoluble oneness with that Divine Life which IS all things. Mysticism cannot obtain in any system of religion which places God and Man in eternal separation as creator and creature, or in which God is eternally transcendental; in short it cannot obtain in any supernatural or dualistic religion without exhibiting a distinct departure therefrom. Dualism and supernaturalism belong to the earlier stages of religion wherein the religious instinct rises no higher than the formal mind, and where, consequently, religious beliefs are more or less grossly materialistic and anthropomorphic. Mysticism must necessarily transcend this, for it commences when the individual is able to escape from the necessitous nature of the formal mind into the higher region of spiritual freedom. This freedom may be a deep and profound *faith*, a *Pistis*, before it becomes a definite attainment, a *Gnôsis*. Thus before Mysticism comes religion as commonly understood at the present time: the 'faith' expressed in a definite belief or creed, and the observance of prescribed ceremonies. This is *exoteric* religion: religion as known historically. It bears the same relation to true spiritual Religion or *quality of life* that the historical evolutionary process of Man does to his true and eternal spiritual nature. It rises from low forms of Fetish worship to gorgeous Ritual performed in stately Temples. At first with fear and trembling, and, later on, in strange Images made with hands, the individual seeks to draw nigh to *That* which in reality he carries in his own inner nature; *That* which is closer and nearer than any external thing. For long and seemingly interminable ages, the individual and the Race retain this false sense of separateness, and man is a pilgrim and a wanderer in the very midst of a *Reality*, ever present, here and now, and of infinite fulness, richness, and bliss. Viewed as a time-process, the great sweep of Cosmic evolution inevitably carries Man forward to the full realisation of his true nature in its oneness with the Absolute; but so long as the sense of separation exists, this progress must take the form of a more or less refined, though always anthropomorphic, concept of a personal Deity, with appropriate forms of propitiatory or laudatory worship; and a necessitous professional class inevitably arises to minister to the demand

15

Exoteric religion is always formal, limited, and thereby exclusive. It finds no truth, no safety outside of its own particular concepts, and these concepts are always more or less crudely realistic, are products of the formal mind, so that spiritual things are thereby conceived of only in terms of time and space.

Esoteric religion and Mysticism, on the other hand, rise into the true region of Spirit, the region of freedom; and we may make this further distinction between these and exoteric religion, that the latter belongs to the region of necessity or law, the others to the region where the soul realises its infinite and inalienable freedom. Life for the individual is necessitous or free just in proportion as it identifies itself on the one hand with form, or on the other hand with principle. Principle, Spirit, can take endless forms and be in nowise bound or limited by any. Life itself, whilst taking on innumerable forms, is essentially free. It is never limited or defined by the form; it is always something more than 'correspondence with environment': though this may be, in a certain sense, the intellectual measure of it, and therefore satisfactory to Science—which is itself necessitous. And since life thus perpetually escapes from and transcends the region of necessity, the region of matter and intellect: shall we not thereby recognise what we intuitively feel in our inmost being, that Life belongs to another order of things than the necessitous; that it is essentially free, and that Freedom exists as the opposite pole of Necessity as certainly as Subject stands opposed to Object.

Subject, or Spirit, is Freedom; Object, or Matter, or Form, is Necessity; but only Necessity when taken as a reality in itself, and as if it were not the veriest outcome and revelation of pure Freedom.

Many attempts have been made by great teachers to raise Religion into this region of Freedom; but the great mass of Humanity is still too materialistic, too much under the sway of the empirical 'reality' of the senses and the formal mind, to be able to appreciate the true inner nature of Religion in its spiritual freedom and spontaneity. Some 1,900 years ago the effort is reputed to have been made by one of the great spiritual teachers of the world; but nothing is sadder in the whole history of Religion than the failure to appreciate the

pure spirituality of the Gospel of Freedom as contained in
the New Testament. No religion has ever held souls in
bondage to the extent that so-called Christianity has done;
no so-called religion has ever resulted in such appalling
crimes.

That the reputed life and teachings of Jesus, as also of the
great Apostle Paul, are profoundly mystical, and intimately
connected with the ancient and pre-existing Gnôsis, is a fact
which research and scholarship is bringing more and more to
light. We might even accord to the Christian Scriptures a
foremost place in the presentation of that Gnôsis; but there
is much work to be done, and probably many other ancient
documents to be discovered, before their real value in this
respect can become generally recognised. In the meanwhile,
as St. Augustine tells us : " The Narratives of the Doctrine are
its cloak. The simple look only at the garment, that is upon
the narrative of the Doctrine; more they know not. The
instructed, however, see not merely the cloak, but what the
cloak covers."

What was known as Gnôsticism in Hellenistic times was
a survival in a more or less corrupt form of pre-Christian
Mysticism. It goes back to Plato and Aristotle and Heraclitus
in Greece, whilst its Eastern sources in Egypt and the Far
East have still to be traced.[1]

" Recent investigations," says the Rev. F. Lamplugh in
the interesting introduction to his English translation of
The Gnôsis of the Light (Codex Brucianus), "have challenged
the traditional outlook and the traditional conclusions and the
traditional 'facts.' With some to-day, and with many more
to-morrow, the burning question is, or will be—not how
did a peculiarly silly and licentious heresy rise within the
Church—but how did the Church rise out of the great
Gnôstic Movement, and how did the dynamic ideas of the
Gnôsis become crystallised into Dogmas ? "

Christian Mysticism will be found to approximate more and
more closely to Gnôsticism the more we discover about the
latter. At present we have only fragmentary records of it,
and these are mostly derived from its ' Christian ' opponents,
who did all they could to misrepresent and ridicule it. " Each
opponent, with the dialectical skill which was common at the

[1] Cf. Mead: *Fragments of a Faith Forgotten.*

time, selected, paraphrased, distorted, and recombined the points which seemed to him to be weakest." [1]

Those who dragged Christianity, or rather the Gnôsis, down from its pure spirituality into a system of materialised dogmas, were naturally bitter foes of a Mysticism which they could not understand, and which appeared to throw discredit upon their own authority as exponents of the relation of God to Man. It is even so to-day; but to-day they have not the power to bind consciences and to stifle knowledge. And so to-day it is the Gnôsis which is reappearing and the theologian who suffers discredit.

The fundamental teaching of the Gnôsis is *the Divine Nature of Man.* At intervals throughout the Dark Ages of ecclesiastical bigotry and dogmatism, has appeared here and there some bright star of mystical knowledge and vision, to proclaim this great truth. God and Man, Man and God: complementary aspects of the One Absolute Immutable Divine Perfection, from which the individual—when he has reached a certain stage of his evolution—is only separated by his own wilful denial, which further experience will correct; for that supreme bliss of union to which here and there a few individual mystics have attained, is the pledge of the potentiality of the real nature of every man coming into this world.

Great as is the mystery for the intellect of the Absolute and the Relative, of Reality and Appearance, of God and Man, of the Word made Flesh, of the Higher and the Lower Self, of Good and Evil—all these being synonyms for the same illimitable and eternal Fact—there is that within us which claims this mystery, this Fact, as the very essence and reason and substance of our being. However small or low or mean or outcast we may appear to be in our individual aspect in the world of Appearances, we have behind or within us, as it were, the other pole of our being; the infinite potentiality of the transcendent and inconceivable richness, and fulness, and glory, and ineffable bliss of the eternal and immeasurable Perfection of the ONE LIFE in Its Absoluteness.

And towards that Perfection all individual things, from atom to man, from man to god, do and must inevitably and

---

[1] Hatch: *The Influence of Greek Ideas and Usages upon the Christian Church,* p. 9.

irresistibly move; sowing and reaping as they go; here sorrow and pain and Dead Sea Fruit; there a measure of joy and gladness, and the ambrosial grain of the Eternal Wheat Fields; drinking now of the bitter waters of Marah, and anon of that Spring of Living Water from which if a man drink he shall assuredly thirst no more.

This is the end of this publication.

Any remaining blank pages are for our book binding
requirements and are blank on purpose.

To search thousands of interesting publications like this one,
please remember to visit our website at:

http://www.kessinger.net

Printed in the United States
111439LV00008B/2/A

9 781425 458119